Letters & Memos—
Just Like That!

Letters & Memos— Just Like That!

Dave Davies

SkillPath Publications

Mission, KS

Project Editor: Kelly Scanlon

Editor: Jane Doyle Guthrie

Creative Director: Rod Hankins

Page Layout: Premila Malik Borchardt

Cover Design: Rod Hankins

ISBN: 1-57294-095-6

Library of Congress Catalog Card Number: 97-67311

10   9   8   7   6   5   4   3   2   1   97   98   99   00   01

Printed in the United States of America

Contents

Introduction

Letters and memos leave a lasting impression, which is why it is so important to produce quality documents.

Letters are more than just words on a page. Presentation, style, and technique can make the difference between success and failure. Everything from the letterhead to the final keystroke helps create an image of you and your organization in the reader's mind, so it had better be good!

And then there are memos. Memos may be for internal consumption only, but they also put your writing abilities under the microscope. As with letters, the right combination of style, tone, and content is needed to get the message across to the reader in a clear and impressive way.

When writing letters or memos, you probably ask yourself some of the following questions:

- What do I really want to say?
- What would be the correct format?
- How do I start?
- Is my argument clear enough?
- Have I said too little, or too much?
- Do I sound too casual, or too formal?
- How should I end it?
- Will it have the desired effect?
- Is it accurate?

Letters & Memos—Just Like That! seeks to answer these questions and many more. You'll find rules and tips to help you create an effective writing style, simple guidelines for correctly formatting documents, and sample documents to illustrate a wide range of letter and memo techniques.

So now what? As with all writing assignments, "procrastination is the thief of time." Let's get started!

Part One
Style

Clichés

Letter writing has a long history, and with the passing of time, certain phrases have come to be used over and over again. These well-worn wordings are known as *clichés* (from a French word meaning "copied").

Why do we use them? Because they're familiar. They come to mind more easily than original thoughts when we're faced with a writing task.

Are they useful? Only if you really want to sound dry and old-fashioned. For a fresh personal style, you should try to replace clichés with phrases of your own.

Hints

1. Be warm and natural.

CLICHÉ: We are in receipt of your communication . . .

BETTER: Thank you for your letter . . .

2. Be direct.

CLICHÉ: Pursuant to our conversation . . .

BETTER: As discussed . . .

3. Don't use padding.

CLICHÉ: Please find enclosed . . .

BETTER: I enclose . . .

4. Make it personal.

CLICHÉ: Please do not hesitate to call . . .

BETTER: Please call me . . .

Exercise

How many clichés can you find in the Wordbound Incorporated letter?

_____

_____

_____

_____

_____

_____

_____

WORDBOUND INCORPORATED

March 2, 2004

John Brown
1661 Endive Street
Greenville, MI 48920

SUBJECT: CLICHÉS

Dear Sir:

We are in receipt of your communication dated February 23, 2004.

Please be advised that, in regard to the above-mentioned subject and pursuant to our subsequent conversation, the matter is receiving attention. In the meantime, please find enclosed the information as requested.

We trust that this meets with your requirements at the present time, and look forward to receiving your further advices. Should you have any questions, please do not hesitate to call.

Yours truly,

M. Bland

M. Bland
Customer Service Manager

72 GREGORY TERRACE • SWORDTON, MO • 64001 • (816) 555-2020

Redundancy

Actually getting started is one of the things we worry about when writing any type of business communication. Covering the page is another.

Often a temptation arises to fill the page faster by using more words, whether they're necessary or not. This leads to the problem of redundancy (from a Latin word meaning "repetition").

Following are some examples of redundancy:

- *In my personal opinion . . .*

  If the opinion is mine, it must be personal—to me! Therefore, *personal* is self-evident.

- *Refer back . . . Combine together . . . Another alternative . . .*

  Re- means "back," *com-* means "together," and *alter-* means "other"; the full meanings are already built into the words.

- *Few in number . . . Brief in duration . . .*

  Logically *few* can only refer to number, and *brief* can only refer to duration.

Hints

1. **Be aware of the redundancy problem.**

2. **Try to say what you have to say as economically as possible.**

3. **Don't use redundant expressions just because they are common (i.e., clichés).**

Exercise

See how many redundant expressions you can find in the Duplocution letter on the next page.

_____

_____

_____

_____

_____

_____

_____

_____

_____

_____

_____

_____

_____

_____

The National Institute of Duplocution

September 10, 2011

Ms. Annabel Lee
1864 Magnolia Terrace
Bluffton, SC 29297

Dear Ms. Lee:

Thank you for ordering a copy of *The Duplocutor's Handbook.*

Unfortunately, we are unable to completely fill your order at this moment in time. The reason is because, despite advance planning, there is no surplus left over in our inventory.

I have, however, gathered together some information that will give you the basic essentials of our program. The consensus of opinion is that the vast majority of what you need to know is therein explained within it.

Past experience indicates that the time needed to reprint the *Handbook* is brief in duration, so after a period of about approximately two weeks, I will return back to you with a copy.

Yours truly sincerely,

W. Longfellow

W. Longfellow
Publicity Manager

6620 Fairway • Redundo Beach, CA 90655 • (805) 555-3331

Formality

Writing letters requires making decisions about formality. Do you want the piece to sound careful, even stiff? Or do you want it to sound relaxed, more like speech?

Formality has to do with the kind of English you use in your letters. Certain words and grammar choices sound formal, while others sound informal.

Formal

- Making a distinction between *who* and *whom*
- Not ending sentences with prepositions
- Not using contractions
- Using elaborate terms (*apprise, dispatch*)

Informal

- Not using *whom*
- Writing sentences the way you would say them
- Using contractions
- Using everyday terms (*get details, send*)

A psychologist might say that an informal style appears more approachable, whereas a formal style seems more professional. Either way, it's important to choose the style that will make the *best impression on your reader*. A customer service organization might choose a less formal style than, say, a legal practice.

Exercise

Compare the two styles in the following letters and decide which writer makes *you* feel more comfortable.

_____

_____

_____

_____

_____

_____

_____

_____

Formal Equipment Incorporated

Dear Sir:

I refer to your letter of June 6, 2007.

The representative with whom you were dealing has apprised me of your present circumstances.

If you would be so kind as to advise me of the exact items to which you are referring, I will be glad to dispatch replacements without further delay.

Informal Equipment Inc.

Dear Sir:

Thank you for your letter of June 6, 2007.

I learned the details of your situation from the representative you were dealing with.

Please let me know exactly which items you need, and I'll have new ones sent right away.

Tone

"The pen is mightier than the sword" is a well-known quotation, but not one you should take to heart if you want good results from your letters and memos!

They say you shouldn't shop for groceries when you're hungry because you'll buy more than you need. The same goes for writing when you're angry: you'll say more than you should! You risk spoiling relations by writing in haste.

Since paper forms a permanent record, you should always think very carefully about how you write to someone. Tempted though you may be to "get tough," the gentle approach usually produces better results.

Hints

1. Remember the "Golden Rule."

Write to others as you would have them write to you.

2. Mind your manners.

"Please" and "thank you" won't increase the cost of your letter— but they might easily make it more profitable!

3. Be positive.

If you adopt a negative tone in your letter, it will create a negative impression in the mind of the reader, and consequently lessen the likelihood of a positive result. Talk "yes"!

Exercise

Compare the two approaches in the letters on the following page and decide which might be more successful.

_____

_____

_____

_____

_____

_____

_____

_____

_____

_____

STRONGARM Collections Limited

Dear Jane White:

This is to advise you that your Creduco Account is over three months in arrears, and has now been passed to us for collection.

If you do not clear the balance within ninety days of the date of this letter, we will have no alternative but to take legal action to recover the money. As you are aware, this will have a negative impact on your credit rating and could prevent you from qualifying for credit in the future.

We expect your response without further delay.

Sunshine Credit Consultants Inc.

Dear Ms. White:

Creduco has passed your overdue account to Sunshine Credit, and it is our pleasure to welcome you as a client.

We understand that unforeseen circumstances can make it difficult to meet payments, and our consultants will be happy to help you create a payment plan that fits your budget. If the balance can be cleared within ninety days, legal action will be avoided, and your credit rating will be unaffected for the future.

Please call us to discuss the matter at your earliest convenience.

Sincerity

No matter how hard you try to "fake" it, people can tell when you're being sincere.

Be careful of "hype" (from the Greek word *hyperbole,* meaning something like "excess"). Don't try to write more than is necessary, appropriate, or even true!

At the other extreme lies understatement—good in moderation, bad if it results in an incomplete message.

Saying too much and saying too little are both counterproductive. One of a writer's responsibilities is to pitch the letter or memo at the right level.

Hints

1. **Always be sincere.**

   If the news is bad, just tell it like it is. Add some empathy or encouragement, but don't try to "sugar the pill."

2. **Be honest.**

   Don't try to hedge an issue; your reader deserves an explanation.

3. **Be clear.**

   Don't try to "blind with science"; your reader may be confused by the terminology, but most people are smart enough to know when they're being bamboozled!

Exercise

What is wrong with the examples on the opposite page?

_____

_____

_____

_____

MEMORANDUM

TO: J. Blow
FROM: Personnel Dept.
DATE: May 6, 2007
SUBJECT: Employment

You will be redundant effective next Monday.

Workhouse Employment Agency Inc.

Dear Mr. Blow:

Thank you for applying with our agency.

Your qualifications and experience are outstanding, and we sincerely appreciate your thinking of us.

Your wonderful résumé will be kept on file for a period of six months, and if anything comes up in that time, we will not hesitate to contact you. Meanwhile, we have little doubt that your considerable talents will find you a suitable position elsewhere.

Yours most sincerely,

A. Workhouse

A. Workhouse

Viewpoint

"What's in it for me?" is a question most people will ask when opening a letter or a memo.

Though it's automatic to write in the *first person* (I, me, my, we, us, our, etc.), as in

I am writing . . . We would like . . . Please send us . . . Call me . . .

the reader, on the other hand, is looking for the *second person* (you, your):

You are requested . . . Your business is appreciated . . .

The question is, which viewpoint should you take?

If you take your readers' viewpoint as much as possible, they'll feel that the message really is for them.

Hints

1. **"You" is what the reader wants to see.**

2. **Put the reader first.**

3. **Make sure there's more "you" than "I" in your letters.**

Exercise

How many first-person references are there in each of the *Goldman* letters on the next page? How many second-person references? Which writer seems more interested in the reader?

_____

_____

_____

_____

_____

_____

_____

_____

_____

A.

Goldman for Groceries

Dear Customer:

We at Goldman are proud to announce the grand opening of our new Superstore.

Our winning formula has made us the first choice of Bellville shoppers, and our Superstore marks the culmination of a year of fantastic growth for us.

We will be opening our doors to shoppers on Saturday at 10 a.m., and the mayor of Bellville will cut the ribbon at noon. Be there to share our joy on this auspicious occasion.

B.

Goldman for Groceries

Dear Customer,

You are warmly invited to the grand opening of the new Goldman Superstore.

Thanks to you and your fellow shoppers, the Superstore marks the culmination of a year of fantastic growth for Goldman in your city.

The doors will be open to welcome you on Saturday at 10 a.m., and the mayor of Bellville will cut the ribbon at noon. Please give Goldman the pleasure of your company on this auspicious occasion.

Organization

"To fail to plan is to plan to fail." For the best results, therefore, you need to plan your letters and memos carefully.

Think of your message as a journey. The subject line or heading, if you have one, is the gateway, and the body forms the road, leading directly to the conclusion. By the time the reader reaches your signature, all that needs to be said should have been said, clearly and concisely. That's the plan!

Letters

Most of your letters should consist of three paragraphs:

- **Paragraph 1**

  Sets the scene: what you are writing about, and why

- **Paragraph 2**

  Provides the details, background, explanation, etc.

- **Paragraph 3**

  Says what you expect to happen next, when and how

Optional:

- **"We look forward . . . "**

  Serves as a smooth bridge to the close

Memos

Memos will normally consist of a subject line plus two paragraphs:

- **Subject**

  Contains the information required to set the scene

- **Paragraph 1**

  Provides background information

- **Paragraph 2**

  Presents the call to action

ASSOCIATION OF BASIC LETTER ORGANIZATIONS

Dear Reader:

We are writing to you either to follow up past correspondence or to introduce a new idea to you now. If you wrote to us, thank you for your letter.

This is what you asked us to do, the information you requested, the details of the product, the explanation for the problem, the reason why you should be interested in what we have to say (i.e., what's in it for you), and all the other things we should be informing you about.

Please do the appropriate thing, such as calling if you need more information, paying the bill, sending us something, returning the enclosed form, or one of a host of other next steps.

We look forward to hearing from or meeting with you, etc.

Yours truly,

MEMORANDUM

ATTN: You

FROM: Us

DATE: Today's

SUBJECT: The Organization of Memos

This paragraph expounds the matter we are dealing with (i.e., the information, assignment, etc., that has been discussed or is a new issue and needs your attention now).

Please do the appropriate thing such as taking some further action, noting our decision, informing someone else, or a host of other possible next steps by a certain time, then report back to us (or not, as the case may be).

The "One Page Rule"

We live in the era of the ten-second sound bite, and the pace of our lives quickens constantly. Now, more than ever, time is at a premium—hence the "One Page Rule."

If someone opens your envelope, there's a good chance they will see your letterhead and glance at your message. But will they turn to a second page? Do they have time? Perhaps, but perhaps not!

The "One Page Rule" says:

Always try to say what you have to say on a single sheet.

Hints

1. **Avoid clichés.**

2. **Cut out redundancy.**

3. **Follow the three-step pattern of letter/memo organization.**

4. **If necessary, use bulleted lists to present information clearly and concisely:**

   - They make it easier for the reader to locate the information.

   - They cut down the wordage.

   - They create white space.

Concise Communications Incorporated

Xxxxx 0, 0000

Xxxxxxxxxxxxxx
Xxxxxxxxxxxxxx
Xxxxxxxxxxx 00000

Dear Reader:

First paragraph—scene setting xxxxxxxxxxx xxxxxxxxxxxx
xxxxxxxxxxxx xxxxx xxxxxxxxxxxx xxxxxxxxxx xxxxxxxxxxxx
xxxxxxxxxxxxxxx Xxxxxxxxxxxxxxxxxx xxxxxx xxxxxxxxxxx xxxxxx
xxxxxxxxx xxxxxxxxxxxxxxxx xxxxxx.

Second paragraph—details xxxxxxxxxxx xxxxxxxx xxxxxx xxx xxxx
xxxxx xxxxxxx and here they are:

- Easy to see
- Brief and to the point
- Restful to the eye

Third paragraph—what happens next xxxxxxxxxxxxxx xxxxxxxxxxxx
xxxxxxxxxxx xxxxxxxxxxxx xxxxxxxxx xxxxxxxxxxxxxxx xxxxxxxxxx.

Yours truly,

Short & Sweet
Directors

The rest of the letterhead without continuation notes, etc.

Sentences and Paragraphs

As stated previously, your basic letter should contain three paragraphs, your basic memo two.

- **What is a paragraph?**

  A paragraph is a group of one or more sentences dealing with a single topic.

- **What is a sentence?**

  A sentence is a group of one or more clauses dealing with a single subject. The sentence begins with a capital letter and ends with a period. Clauses are usually separated by commas.

- **What is a clause?**

  A clause is a group of related words that includes an action (verb) and usually the person or thing responsible for the action (subject).

Hints

1. Paragraphs

- One-sentence paragraphs are acceptable style. As long as you include all the essential information, short is good.

- State the topic in the first sentence of each paragraph to let the reader know what to expect.

2. Sentences

- Keep sentences short—maximum three clauses. A two-clause sentence averages twelve words—the ideal length.

- Beware of overpunctuating. Fewer clauses equals fewer commas.

- Make sure every sentence has a verb.

Exercise

Spot the six mistakes in the Accurate construction letter on the next page.

1. _____

   _____

2. _____

   _____

3. _____

   _____

4. _____

   _____

5. _____

   _____

6. _____

   _____

ACCURATE CONSTRUCTION INC.

August 6, 2007

Bill Black
Bill Black the Builder Ltd.
3829 Brick Lane
Rawlings, MT 59291

Dear Mr. Black:

Thank you for your letter of August 3, which I received yesterday, having previously closed the file on our correspondence, your payment being more than ninety days overdue, to put the matter in the hands of the collection agency.

- A check for the outstanding balance
- A guarantee from a bank or other financial institution
- Payment in advance is what we will need before your account can be reinstated.

These matters regrettable. We value, our customers, and do what we can, to avoid legal problems. I sincerely hope we can in the future.

Look forward to hearing from you.

Barry Blue

Barry Blue
Credit Manager

795 MORTAR • BRICKTON, MT 59290 • (406) 555-0011

Accuracy

Your correspondence provides others with a measure of your credibility, so it has to convey a high standard.

Accuracy is one of the more obvious indicators of quality. Consumers express reactions such as "The product sounds good, but the typos worry me!" That logic is sound. That is, editing and proofreading are quality controls; if these steps are missing, what other controls are being sacrificed in the making of the product?

You should think about accuracy on the following levels:

- **Factual accuracy**

  Get the facts straight. Know what you're writing about.

- **Grammatical accuracy**

  Keep your sentences short.

  Keep them clear.

  Keep them complete.

  Make the punctuation logical.

- **Drafting accuracy**

  Avoid typographic errors (typos).

  Avoid spelling errors.

  Use the spellcheck function on your word processor, but don't rely on it.

Two precautions are necessary to ensure accuracy:

- *Editing:* reading over the correspondence yourself or having others read it to check accuracy and style.

- *Proofreading:* checking drafts for typos and spelling mistakes.

Exercise

Find the ten mistakes in Anne White's letter on the following page.

1. _____
   _____

2. _____
   _____

3. _____
   _____

4. _____
   _____

5. _____
   _____

6. _____
   _____

7. _____
   _____

8. _____
   _____

9. _____
   _____

10. _____
    _____

CAREFREE INDUSTRIES INCORPORATED

July 4, 2005

Ms. Jane Jones
49 main Street
Enniston, NJ 07019

Dear Ms. Jones;

I recieved your letter of June 31.

Thank you for inviting Mr. John Smith to attend your convention.

Unfortunatly Mr. Smith is away on buisness in New York, but, as soon as he return from the nation's capital I am sure he will give your letter his immediate attention.

Sincerly,

Anne White

Ann White
P.A. to John Smith

21 BUTTERFLY COURT • GARDENS, GA 30060 • (770) 555-4321

Part Two
Formatting Your Letters

Parts of a Letter

The first step in formatting your letters is to make sure you know all the parts of a letter and where they belong. Review not only the terms but the function each performs.

Exercise

Match letter parts A-M with positions 1-13 as tagged on the next page (1 is already done for you):

A. Administrative notations =

B. Attention line =

C. Body of the letter =

D. Complimentary close =

E. Date =

F. Delivery notations =

G. Inside address =

H. Letterhead = **1**

I. Postscript =

J. Reference line =

K. Salutation =

L. Signature block =

M. Subject line =

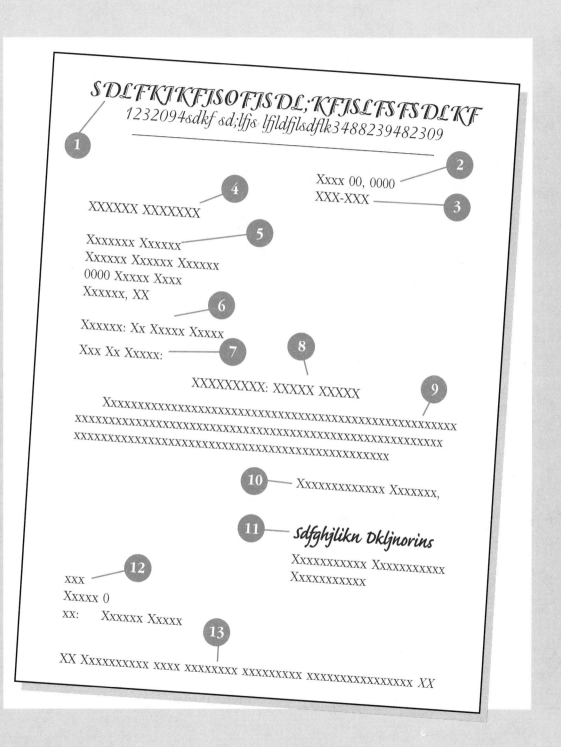

Letterhead

Your letterhead is a very important part of your corporate image, intended to communicate the organization in an impressive and artistic way.

The letterhead will usually contain the following elements:

- Logo
- Full name of the organization
- Full street address, including suite or building number
- Post office box number
- City, state, and ZIP code
- Telephone and fax numbers
- E-mail address

Executive letterhead may also contain "Office of the Vice President" or some such personalized information.

The letterhead may be centered, spread from margin to margin, or concentrated to one side of the page. All the information may be at the head, or it may be divided between head and foot.

Conventional style suggests that a letter should look like a picture, with the margins as the frame. Always try to work with your letterhead to create that pleasing picture.

Hints

1. **Make your letter look balanced.**

   Set your margins to fit the letterhead if possible.

2. **Don't crowd the letterhead.**

   Leave at least three lines between the letterhead and the letter.

3. **Leave plenty of white space on the page.**

   This visual detail is restful to the eye.

4. **For multipage letters that require continuation sheets, use letterhead only for the first page!**

   If you have to break the "One Page Rule," use continuation sheets with headings as shown on the following pages.

Letterhead

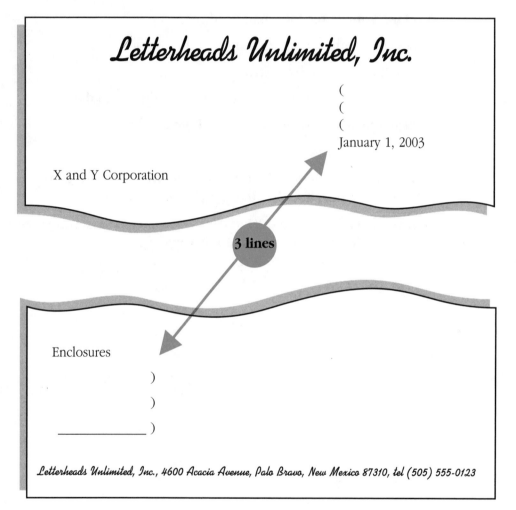

Letterheads Unlimited, Inc.

(
(
(
January 1, 2003

X and Y Corporation

3 lines

Enclosures

)
)
_____)

Letterheads Unlimited, Inc., 4600 Acacia Avenue, Palo Bravo, New Mexico 87310, tel (505) 555-0123

Continuation Sheet Headings

a. Block Letter Format

Page 2
X and Y Corporation
January 1, 2003

b. Modified Letter Formats

X and Y Corporation   -2-   January 1, 2003

Date Line

The first line in a business letter is the date.

There are four standard positions for the date line:

- Blocked left
- Centered
- Blocked right
- Five or ten spaces right of center

The usual sequence is month-day-year: January 1, 2003

Exceptions appear in U.S. military communications and in some overseas countries, where you'll see the day-month-year sequence: 1 January, 2003

More on Dates

Here is how dates should appear in the body of the letter (note when commas are used):

- the first of January through the thirty-first of August
- January 1 through August 31
- August 31, 2004
- 8/1/04
- On August 31, 2004, we wrote you
- We last wrote you in August 2004
- On August 31, we received your reply

Block Layout:

Dreamtime Dating Service Incorporated

January 1, 2003

Modified Layouts:

Dreamtime Dating Service Incorporated

January 1, 2003

Dreamtime Dating Service Incorporated

January 1, 2003

Dreamtime Dating Service Incorporated

January 1, 2003

Reference Line and Delivery Notations

Reference Line

The reference line exists to help a busy office locate a file more efficiently.

It might consist of:

- An account number.

- A policy number.

- Some combination of initials, date, and serial number that you've been asked to include in correspondence or that you need for your own filing system.

The reference line normally is typed directly below the date or centered four lines lower. It appears on the first page and on any continuation sheets.

Delivery Notations

If a special method of delivery is used, write it on the envelope; for example:

- AIRMAIL

- BY HAND

- CERTIFIED MAIL

- REGISTERED

- SPECIAL DELIVERY

Certain restrictions can be added where necessary, such as:

- CONFIDENTIAL

- PERSONAL

- CLASSIFIED

You also can make these notations in the letter, below the date line and above the inside address.

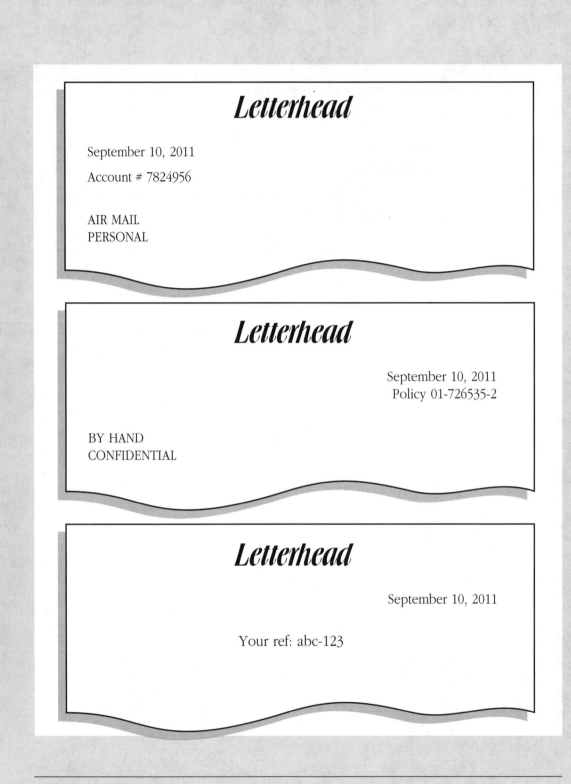

Letterhead

September 10, 2011

Account # 7824956

AIR MAIL
PERSONAL

Letterhead

September 10, 2011
Policy 01-726535-2

BY HAND
CONFIDENTIAL

Letterhead

September 10, 2011

Your ref: abc-123

Inside Address

The inside address consists of the following elements:

- The addressee's courtesy title and full name

- The addressee's position, if necessary

- The full name of the organization

- The full street address

- City, state, and ZIP code

Hints

1. **Don't use courtesy titles before *and* after the adressee's name.**

   WRONG: Dr. Joan B. Smith, M.D.

   RIGHT: Joan B. Smith, M.D. *or* Dr. Joan B. Smith

2. **Don't try to shorten or otherwise change the addressee's position or the name of the organization (check previous correspondence if in doubt).**

3. **In street addresses, use numerals for all numbers except "One."**

4. **In numbered street names, use words instead of numerals for *First Street* through *Twelfth Street*.**

5. **Most writers use numerals from *13th Street* on, though some continue to spell them out, as in *Forty-second Street*.**

6. **Where there is an apartment or suite number, do not use *Number, No.,* or *#*.**

7. Do not abbreviate directional points (e.g., North, West, etc.) when they appear before a street name. When used after a street name, compound directional points such as Northeast may be abbreviated (e.g., NE).

8. Do not use ampersands in a street address.

9. Do not abbreviate address elements such as Avenue, Road, and Street in an inside address.

Exercise

Spot the eight mistakes in the reply on the next page.

1. _____

2. _____

3. _____

4. _____

5. _____

6. _____

7. _____

8. _____

I look forward to hearing from you.

Yours truly,

Edward Barnes

Edward Barnes, M.Sc.
President, Clinical Division

Gamma Pharmaceutical Products Limited, 400 College Way, Unit 3, Columbia, WA 98290 (360) 555-3168

Accurate Consulting Incorporated

July 8, 2009

Mr. Edwin Barnes, M.S.C.
Chairman, Clinical Department
Gamma Pharmaceuticals Ltd.
400 College Way, Unit # Three
Columbia, WA 73890

Subject Line

The subject line sums up the contents of a letter in a few words, providing an instant focus for the reader and making filing easier.

Capitalization

There are three alternatives:

- ALL IN CAPITALS
- Capitalized key words (with or without boldface or underlining)
- Capitalized first word only (with or without boldface or underlining)

Introducing the Subject Line

There are several alternatives:

- Subject:
- Subj:
- Sub:
- Reference:
- Ref:
- Re:
- NO INTRODUCTION

Positions

- Before salutation
- In place of salutation (simplified letter)
- After salutation

Hints

1. **Make subject lines short and to the point.**
2. **Don't write full sentences—use key words only.**
3. **The subject line may be blocked left or centered.**

Roberta Wood
Wood Construction Company
3729 Elm Street
Frampton, IL 61236

Dear Ms. Wood:

<u>Re: Softwood lumber supply</u>

Regarding our recent discussions, this is to confirm that a consignment of
Oregon spruce has been prepared for shipment. . . .

Samuel Horn
Kansas Meat Packers Ltd.
6969 Squabb Road
Masson, KS 66192

Subject: Refrigeration Upgrade

Dear Mr. Horn:

Thank you for your inquiry. . . .

Faculty of Sciences
Columbia College
2945 Ivy Avenue
Columbia, NE 68315

SUMMER EDUCATION PROGRAMS

We would like to inform the Columbia College Faculty of Sciences that a
new schedule of programs will be available. . . .

Salutation

The salutation, like the complimentary close, is a very old tradition in letter writing. "Dear Sir" and "Dear Madam" are still going strong, even though they originated in the era of knights in shining armor, when the world was a very different place! These days "Madam" sounds strange to some people, and in the modern workplace it is no longer reasonable to salute all executives as "Dear Sir."

Here are some salutation alternatives:

- **Name unknown, gender known**

Dear Sir	Gentlemen	
Dear Madam	Ladies	Ladies and Gentlemen

- **Name and gender known**

Dear Ms. Smith	Dear Mrs. Brown
Dear Mr. Jones	Dear Miss Green

- **Name known, gender unknown**

  Dear Leslie White   Dear T.J. Redd

- **Name and gender unknown**

  Dear Sir or Madam

  To Whom It May Concern (sounds a little cold, even hostile!)

  By category of addressee:

Dear Resident	Dear Doctors
Dear Colleague	Dear Friends

- **No salutation, subject line only**

Exercise

Add suitable salutations to follow the inside addresses below.

A. Dr. A. Cutt and Dr. B. Thrust
   Sterile Surgical Inc.
   2800 Langerhans Parkway
   Medville, VA 23293

   _____

B. Marion Morrissey
   620 Wayne Drive, Suite 501
   Vallance, NM 87012

   _____

C. The Governors
   Waywood School
   900 Pleasant Valley Highway
   Schoolville, CA 94456

   _____

D. Clytemnestra Brown (Mrs.)
   96 Martin Luther King Highway
   Jonestown, MS 38573

   _____

E. The Belton Men's Association
   4900 Beltway
   Belton, PA 19210

   _____

Complimentary Close

Once upon a time (and still in some countries, notably France), it was usual to end business letters something like this:

and we respectfully pray that you, Sir, accept this submission of our

humble assurances that we remain,

Your sincere and dedicated servants,

etc.

The above has gradually shrunk to something like "Yours sincerely."

Some people question the relevance of affectionate expressions like "Dear" and "Sincerely" in business correspondence. The answer? Convention.

Which Complimentary Close?

Very formal:	Respectfully	Respectfully yours	
Polite:	Yours truly	Very truly yours	
Medium:	Yours sincerely	Sincerely yours	Sincerely
Friendly:	Cordially	Cordially yours	
Informal:	Regards	Yours	Best wishes

Exercise

Fill gaps A–E below with closes 1–5:

1. Cordially yours
2. Respectfully
3. Best wishes
4. Yours truly
5. Sincerely

I look forward to receiving your response to this complaint as soon as possible.

   A. _____

So, old buddy, let's hear from you soon.

   B. _____

We look forward to seeing you in Townsville again when you bring the next order.

   C. _____

And the Ambassador may rest assured we will take prompt action.

   D. _____

Thank you again for your service, and we look forward to doing business in the future.

   E. _____

Signature Block and Administrative Notations

Signature Block

The signature block consists of:

- Signature
- Name of signatory

It can also include the signatory's business title and department if these are not printed on the letterhead.

Administrative Notations

The administrative notations that appear below the signature block include:

- **Typist's, or writer's and typist's, initials** (writer in capitals, typist in lowercase)

  abc   DEF/abc   DEF:abc

- **Enclosure notation**

  Enclosure   Enclosures (2)   Enc. 2   enc.   encl.

- **Copy notation**

  c   cc   cc: Copy to

Exercise

Use the following information to fill gaps A–E in the letter on the next page:

- Dr. Winston Smith wrote the letter but was unable to sign it.

- Judy Harrison is the personal assistant to Dr. Smith.

- Wanda May Hancock was the typist.

- Five additional documents were enclosed.

- A copy was sent to Dr. William Jones.

Massachusetts School of Internal Medicine

November 10, 2011

Dr. Harvey Whyte
College of Physicians
200 Greytowers Road
Boston, MA 01271

Dear Dr. Whyte:

Thank you for agreeing to chair the forthcoming conference on Aggravation of the Lower Bowel and Other Pernicious Disorders.

Dr. Smith wonders if you would care to join him and Dr. William Jones for a review of the enclosed discussion papers at some point during the next two weeks. If so, please suggest a time that is convenient.

Yours sincerely,

Judy Harrison

A. _____

B. _____

C. _____

D. _____

E. _____

10 Paul Revere Way   Boston, MA 01277   (617) 555-6973

Postscript

Postcripts (*post* = after, *script* = what is written) are added to your document as an afterthought, and appear last.

There are two views on postscripts:

- **Should a postscript be necessary at all?**

  A well-planned, well-written letter covers all the relevant information within the body, so a postscript is superfluous.

- **What about a parting shot?**

  Sometimes you can lull your reader into a false sense of security and then use a postscript to really get your point across.

As always, the most important question is, how will it affect the reader?

If you add a postscript:

- Treat it as a regular paragraph (i.e., blocked or indented like the others).

- Add the letters P.S. or leave them out—they are not actually necessary.

- Initial the postscript.

Coups D'Escalier, Société Anonyme

February 3, 2004

John Deer
Marketing Director
Consumer Supplies Limited
400 Industrial Lane
Hartwell, MI 48901

Dear Sir:

This is to inform you that Coups D'Escalier, S.A., will no longer be dealing with Consumer Supplies Limited, due to the consistently inferior quality of your merchandise.

Truly yours,

Pat Stoney

Pat Stoney
President

P.S. Do not expect payment for the last consignment. *PS*

P.P.S. In case you are contemplating legal action, too late—we are already in receivership. *PS*

01-04 Rue Road   Ste. Genevieve, MO 63671   (314) 555-8899

Simplified Letter

The simplified letter resembles the block letter, with the following differences:

- No salutation
- No complimentary close
- Reduced number of keystrokes

Subject Line

A subject line, all in capitals, replaces the salutation.

Name - Title

These appear below the signature on one line, uppercase and separated by a dash or comma.

Hints

1. **The addressee is usually mentioned in the first and last paragraphs.**

CRAFTWAY PUBLICATIONS

January 1, 2002

Ann Lerner
Director
Education Exchange
1 School Lane
Cunningham, MT 59634

SIMPLIFIED LETTER

Ms. Lerner, xxxxxxx xxxxxxxxx xxxxxxxxx xxxxx xxxxxxxxx xxxxxxxxx
xxxxxxxxx xxxxxxx xxxxx xxxx xxxxx xxxxxxxxx.

Xxxxxx xxxxxxx xxxxxxxxx xxxxxxxxx xxxxx xxxxx xxx xxxxxxxx xxxx xxx xxx
xxxxxxxx xxxxx xxxx xxxxx x x xxxxxxxx xxxxx xxxxx xxxxx xxxxxx.

Finally, Ms. Lerner, xxxxxxx xxxxxx xxxxxxx xxxxxx xxxxxx xxxxx
xxxxx xxxxx xxxxx xxxxx xxxxxx xxxxx xxx xxxxxxxxx.

David Livingstone

DAVID LIVINGSTONE - PRESIDENT

wmh
enc. 2

c: Dr. S. T. Smith

16 BEAR HOLLOW • MOUNTAIN VIEW, KENTUCKY 40204 • (502) 555-6251

Block Letter With Open Punctuation

Block Letter

The block letter has the following features:

- All parts typed flush with the left margin
- No indents (except for quoted material)
- Paragraphs spaced

Open Punctuation

Following are the main features of open punctuation:

- No period after date
- No punctuation at line ends in inside address (except for abbreviations)
- Salutation unpunctuated
- Complimentary close unpunctuated
- Signature block unpunctuated

CRAFTWAY PUBLICATIONS

January 1, 2002

Ann Lerner
Director
Education Exchange
1 School Lane
Cunningham, MT 59634

Dear Ms. Lerner

Subject: Block Letter with Open Punctuation

Xxxxxxx xxxxxxxxx xxxxxxxxx xxxxx xxxxxxxxx xxxxxxxxx xxxxxxxx
xxxxxxx xxxxx xxxx xxxxxx xxxxxxxxx.

Xxxxxx xxxxxxx xxxxxxxx:

     Xxxxxxxxx xxxxxx xxxxx xxxxxxx xxxxxxxxx xxxxxxx xxxxx

     xxxxxxx xxxxxxx xxxxxx xxxxxxxx xxxxxxxx xxxxxxx xxx.

Xxxxxxxxxxx xxxxx xxxxxxx xxxxxx xxxx xxxxx xxxxx xxxxx xxxxxxx.

Very truly yours

David Livingstone

David Livingstone
President

Modified Block Letter With Mixed Punctuation

Modified Block Letter

Four differences distinguish the modified block letter from the block letter:

- Position of date
- Position of complimentary close
- Position of signature block
- Continuation sheet headings (see "Letterhead," page 40)

Mixed Punctuation

The main features of mixed punctuation are as follows:

- No period after date
- No punctuation of line ends in inside address (except for abbreviations)
- Colon after salutation
- Unpunctuated complimentary close
- Unpunctuated signature block line ends

CRAFTWAY PUBLICATIONS

January 1, 2002

Ann Lerner
Director
Education Exchange
1 School Lane
Cunningham, MT 59634

Dear Ms. Lerner:

Subject: Modified Block Letter With Mixed Punctuation

Xxxxxxxxxxxxx xxxxxxxx xxxxxxx xxxxxx xxxx xxxxxx xxxxxxxxx.

Xxxxxx xxxxxxx xxxxxxxxxx xxxxx xxxxx xxx xxxxxxxx xxxx xxx xxx xxxxxxxx xxxxx xxxx xxxxx x x xxxxxxxxx xxxxx xxx xxxxxx xxxxxx.

Xxxxxxxxxxx xxxxxx xxxxxxx xxxxxx xxxxxx xxxxx xxxxx xxxxx xxxxx xxxxx xxxxxx xxxxx xxx.

Very truly yours

David Livingstone

David Livingstone
President

wmh
enc. 2

c: Dr. S. T. Smith

16 BEAR HOLLOW • MOUNTAIN VIEW, KENTUCKY 40204 • (502) 555-6251

Modified Semi-Block Letter With Closed Punctuation

Modified Semi-Block Letter

The modified semi-block letter differs from the modified block letter in two ways:

- Paragraphs are indented.
- Postscript is indented.

Closed Punctuation

The following features distinguish closed punctuation:

- Period after date
- Fully punctuated inside address
- Colon after salutation
- Comma after complimentary close
- Punctuated signature block
- Punctuated administrative notations

CRAFTWAY PUBLICATIONS

January 1, 2002.

Ann Lerner,
Director,
Education Exchange,
1 School Lane,
Cunningham, MT 59634.

Dear Ms. Lerner:

Subject: Modified Semi-Block Letter With Closed Punctuation

Xxxxxxx xxxxxxxxx xxxxxxxxx xxxxx xxxxxxxxx xxxxxxxxx xxxxxx
xxxxxx xxxxx xxxx xxxxxx xxxxxxxxx.

Xxxxxxxxxxxx xxxxxx xxxxxxx xxxxxx xxxxxx xxxxx xxxxx xxxxx
xxxxx xxxxxxxxx xxxxxxx xxxxx xxxxx xxx.

Sincerely yours,

David Livingstone

David Livingstone,
President.

wmh
enc. 2,

c: Dr. S. T. Smith.

P.S. Xxxxxxx xxxxx xxxxx xxxxx xxxxx xxxxxx. *DL*

Part Three
Sample Letters

Inquiry

The letter of inquiry is a request for information. Like most effective letters, it is short and to the point.

Basic Structure

Paragraph 1

Provides background, what writer is trying to do

Paragraph 2

Expresses what writer would like to know

Paragraph 3

Presents the call to action—what to do and when

Key Phrases (not clichés!)

"We are planning/researching/etc. . . . "

"Please send (the following information) . . . "

"Your early response will be appreciated . . . "

APEX Agency Services Inc.

2600 Brooklands Drive, Mount Morris, NC 28097 Tel: (704) 555-2345 Fax: (704) 555-2346

February 2, 2003

The Manager
Office Warehouse
762 Broadway
Mount Morris, NC 28098

Dear Sir or Madam:

MODULAR OFFICE FURNITURE

We are planning to move to new premises later this year and would like to replace our existing office furniture with a new modular system.

Would you please send us a full information package on the modular office furniture you supply, including details of:

- Available color schemes.
- Warranty terms.
- Price with any possible discounts.

Since our new lease will be effective April 1, your early response will be appreciated.

Truly yours,

Donna Middlemiss

Donna Middlemiss
Director

DMM/wmh

Response

The response to a letter of inquiry serves two purposes:

- To confirm transmittal of the necessary information
- Where appropriate, to sell

Basic Structure

Paragraph 1

Expresses thanks for inquiry and notes that information is enclosed

Paragraph 2

Any relevant supporting information, including sales pitch

Paragraph 3

Expresses hope that this answers the question or offers further help, information, etc., as required

Key Phrases

"Thank you for your . . . "

"I enclose . . . "

"I hope this answers/helps . . . "

"If you need any further information, please . . . "

office warehouse

762 Broadway - Mount Morris, N.C. 28098 - (704) 555-5711

February 10, 2003

Donna Middlemiss
Director
APEX Agency Services Inc.
2600 Brooklands Drive
Mount Morris, NC 28097

Dear Ms. Middlemiss:

Re: Modular Office Furniture

Thank you for your inquiry dated February 2. I enclose the latest edition of the Modutech catalog, which includes full details of warranty terms and available color schemes, together with a current price list.

We have represented Modutech for several years, and our clients have expressed a high level of satisfaction. Units are durable and well-finished, and I am confident you will not find a better product in the price range.

Please call me if you need any other information, or visit our showroom and allow me to introduce you to Modutech in person.

Sincerely yours,

Alice Springs

Alice Springs
Sales Manager

AS/sap
Enclosure

Order

One thing all orders seem to have in common is *urgency*. Having waited until the last moment to make a decision, most people need it filled yesterday!

Basic Structure

Paragraph 1

Presents the order, plus check, charge, credit, etc., information

Paragraph 2

Lays out details of the order clearly (including quantity, description, price, and total) if no order form is attached

Paragraph 3

Asks for a quick response

Key Phrases

"Please accept . . ."

"We would be grateful if . . . as quickly as possible"

APEX Agency Services Inc.

2600 Brooklands Drive, Mount Morris, NC 28097 Tel: (704) 555-2345 Fax: (704) 555-2346

February 28, 2003

Alice Springs
Sales Manager
Office Warehouse
762 Broadway
Mount Morris, NC 28098

Dear Ms. Springs:

MODUTECH FURNITURE

Please accept this order for immediate shipment to the above address, with 90 days' credit as agreed:

Quantity	Description	Unit Price	Total
2	Modutech "Executive" Unit B, biscuit	$795.99	$1,591.98
4	Modutech "Admin" Unit F, slate	$495.99	$1,983.96
		Total	$3,575.94

Since we have barely one month before opening for business on April 1, we would be grateful if this order could be handled as quickly as possible.

Truly yours,

Donna Middlemiss

Donna Middlemiss
Director

DMM/wmh

Partial Delivery

A partial delivery is a major inconvenience. The letter has to show that you are doing what you can to meet the customer's urgent needs. It's also a good idea to resell the merchandise: if a thing is worth having, it's worth waiting for!

Basic Structure

Paragraph 1

Expresses thanks for the order

Paragraph 2

Identifies what can be sent now

Paragraph 3

Notes what is missing and to follow as soon as possible

Key Phrases

"Unfortunately, due to . . . "

"These items have been back ordered . . . "

"Expect delivery within . . . "

office warehouse

762 Broadway - Mount Morris, N.C. 28098 - (704) 555-5711

March 5, 2003

Donna Middlemiss
Director
APEX Agency Services Inc.
2600 Brooklands Drive
Mount Morris, NC 28097

Dear Ms. Middlemiss:

Thank you for your order dated February 28. Office Warehouse is delighted to welcome you as a customer.

Your four units of Modutech Admin F are scheduled for immediate delivery, and our shipping department should by now have contacted you to arrange a convenient time.

Unfortunately, due to the extreme popularity of the Modutech Line, we are temporarily out of Executive B units. I have placed an urgent back order with our national distribution center, and we expect to receive the items within two weeks at the very most. Please be assured that the units will be rushed to you as soon as possible.

Sincerely yours,

Alice Springs

Alice Springs
Sales Manager

AS/sap

Complaint

Letters of complaint are sometimes necessary and should be composed of the following elements to get the desired result (i.e., an adjustment and an apology):

- A measured sense of outrage—not too harsh, not too mild
- A detailed account of events, not leaving out any material information
- A clear statement of what you expect

The contents of complaint letters will differ widely according to the problem, but the structure is universal.

Basic Structure

Paragraph 1

Introduces or gives background to the complaint

Paragraph 2

Describes events surrounding the complaint itself

Paragraph 3

Expresses disappointment/surprise, effect on business relationship, and what is expected to rectify the situation

APEX Agency Services Inc.

2600 Brooklands Drive, Mount Morris, NC 28097 Tel: (704) 555-2345 Fax: (704) 555-2346

March 15, 2003

Alice Springs
Sales Manager
Office Warehouse
762 Broadway
Mount Morris, NC 28098

Dear Ms. Springs:

MODUTECH ADMIN UNIT F FURNITURE

On March 8 your shipping people delivered four Modutech Admin F furniture units to our premises. This was a partial fulfillment of our order dated February 28. We are still waiting for the balance of the order, even though our opening is only two weeks away.

When the units were delivered, we were surprised to find that there was an extra charge for assembly, even though there was no mention of this in your catalog or price list. Moreover, after the crew had spent two hours assembling the units, they still seemed unstable, with loose screws and ill-fitting drawers.

As a result of the late delivery, the hidden costs, and the poor assembly quality, we are very disappointed in the service we have received so far from Office Warehouse. If you wish to retain our business, please cancel any assembly charges and ensure our order is completed without further delay.

Truly yours,

Donna Middlemiss

Donna Middlemiss
Director

DMM/wmh

Adjustment

The letter of adjustment provides "damage control." It must be polite and written in the spirit of "the customer is always right."

Basic Structure

Paragraph 1

Expresses thanks for identifying the situation and acknowledges bad news

Paragraph 2

Offers explanation (or excuse!)

Paragraph 3

Describes adjustment (i.e., promises to do what was asked and requests that this not spoil business relationship)

Key Phrases

"Thank you for bringing this to our attention/informing us/letting us know, etc. . . . "

"We regret/are sorry for the inconvenience/misunderstanding, etc. . . . "

"Allow me to explain . . . "

"Please accept our apology . . . "

"You are a valued customer . . . "

"We value your business . . . "

"Your business is important to us . . . "

"I assure you that in the future . . ."

"Please let us know how we can improve the service . . . "

office warehouse

762 Broadway - Mount Morris, N.C. 28098 - (704) 555-5711

March 20, 2003

Donna Middlemiss
Director
APEX Agency Services Inc.
2600 Brooklands Drive
Mount Morris, NC 28097

Dear Ms. Middlemiss:

Thank you for letting me know about the assembly problems with your Modutech furniture units. We regret the inconvenience, especially as it comes at such a busy time for your company.

What happened was an unfortunate misunderstanding, which I would like to clarify without further delay. In order to get the units to you as quickly as possible, our shipping department hired a temporary crew who were unfamiliar with our products and policies.

Let me assure you that Office Warehouse values your business and that your Executive B units are now ready to be shipped. I will have our permanent crew not only deliver and assemble them but also check the assembly of your Admin F units, at no charge. Once again, we apologize for the inconvenience.

Sincerely yours,

Alice Springs

Alice Springs
Sales Manager

Payment Request

Payment request letters are unpopular both to send and receive.

Recipients don't like them because they bring escalating pressure with each round. Senders don't like them because they usually mark the start of a long, drawn-out correspondence, often ending with a collection agency.

Basic Structure

Paragraph 1

Provides notification that payment is overdue

Paragraph 2

Explains what to do now

Paragraph 3

Requests avoiding problems and "staying friends"

Hints

What you don't want is to have the receiver ignore payment requests. Many writers start with an "attention grabber," such as one of the following:

- **Question**

  Have you ever had to send a payment reminder?

- **Colorful line**

  The leaves are already falling from the trees, and you haven't paid your spring installment yet!

- **Strong headline**

  OVERDUE ACCOUNT

office warehouse

762 Broadway - Mount Morris, N.C. 28098 - (704) 555-5711

July 25, 2003

Donna Middlemiss
Director
APEX Agency Services Inc.
2600 Brooklands Drive
Mount Morris, NC 28097

Dear Ms. Middlemiss:

RE: OVERDUE ACCOUNT

On March 21, 2003, you received the final installment of an order for Modutech modular office furniture. The total value of the order was $3,575.94, on agreed terms of 90 days' credit. A notice was sent May 15 reminding you that payment was due on June 21, but so far no payment has been received.

Our ability to offer credit terms to our valued clients depends on their cooperation in paying on schedule. We would therefore be grateful if you could settle this account as soon as possible.

Perhaps your payment is already on its way, in which case please overlook this letter. If on the other hand there are difficulties affecting your ability to pay, please let us know. We will do what we can to ensure that your account stays in good standing and help preserve your credit rating for the future.

Sincerely yours,

Norris Coles

Norris Coles
Business Manager

Collection

At the collection stage, the temptation is to get tough—what's left to lose?

The answer is "the money." You'll only get a fraction of what you're owed if the file goes to a collection agency. What you are hoping for is a last-minute change of heart.

Basic Structure

Paragraph 1

Acknowledges ignoring efforts to collect

Paragraph 2

Provides a last warning

Paragraph 3

Requests payment to avoid unpleasantness that otherwise must follow

Hints

1. Be fair.

You know they owe you money; they know it too. By taking a reasonable tone, you might appeal to their sense of fair play.

2. Be polite.

Saying "please" doesn't actually cost anything, and it may just do the trick.

3. Be positive.

Talk "yes," and emphasize the benefits of paying up: avoiding legal problems, staying friends, etc.

office warehouse

762 Broadway - Mount Morris, N.C. 28098 - (704) 555-5711

September 20, 2003

Donna Middlemiss
Director
APEX Agency Services Inc.
2600 Brooklands Drive
Mount Morris, NC 28097

Dear Ms. Middlemiss:

OVERDUE ACCOUNT - FINAL NOTICE

Despite frequent reminders, I note with regret that your account for $3,665.74 (including interest) is still outstanding.

I must therefore make this final request for immediate settlement of the account.

At Office Warehouse we value all our customers. However, unless I hear from you within seven days, your account will be passed to a collection agency with the usual consequences. Please help me avoid this unpleasant step by giving the matter your urgent attention.

Sincerely yours,

Norris Coles

Norris Coles
Business Manager

Credit Refusal

As with any "bad news" letter, a credit refusal must be tactfully handled. You don't want to lose money to bad credit, but you don't want to lose the sale either!

Basic Structure

Paragraph 1

Expresses thanks for applying for credit

Paragraph 2

States with regret that the answer is "no," and why

Paragraph 3

Encourages customer to pay cash or show some other reason credit should be granted

Key Phrases

"Thank you for you order . . . "

"We appreciate your business . . . "

"We have reviewed your application . . . "

"I regret to inform you/I am sorry to say . . . "

"On the basis of the information . . . "

"If there is any other information . . . "

"We will be happy to review . . . "

"Meanwhile, there is cash, plus discount, etc. . . . "

Homebuilders Hardware

5000 North Ringway, Rookwell, ID 83465 (208) 555-0345

June 7, 2008

Mr. Harry Bloy
Harry Bloy Construction Limited
5920 Dry Creek Lane
Rockwell, ID 83460

Dear Mr. Bloy:

Thank you for placing your order with Homebuilders Hardware. We certainly appreciate your business, and look forward to serving you in the future.

Your application for 90 days' credit has been reviewed, and I regret to inform you that, on the basis of the credit information we have seen so far, we are unable to comply. Your company already has some substantial commitments, and we would not wish to add to them.

However, if there is any other financial information you could present to us, we would certainly reconsider the matter. In the meantime, we will be happy to offer you a 10% trade discount on your cash purchases.

Cordially yours,

Ed Marley

Ed Marley
Credit Manager

EBM/tgf

Credit Cancellation

This is another "bad news" letter, requiring the three magic ingredients:

- Tact
- Justification
- Hope

Basic Structure

Paragraph 1

Emphasizes the value of customer's business

Paragraph 2

Mentions nonpayment of bills and expresses need to suspend credit

Paragraph 3

Offers some assistance and hope for a positive outcome

Hints

1. **You don't want to lose the customer.**
2. **You don't want the account to go to collection.**

Homebuilders Hardware

5000 North Ringway, Rookwell, ID 83465 (208) 555-0345

June 8, 2008

Mr. Dan Durham
DD Homes Inc.
9209 Sunnyhills Crescent
Rockwell, ID 83457

Dear Dan:

For some years you have been one of our best customers, maintaining your account in good standing through prompt and regular payments.

Unfortunately, things have been slow in the construction sector lately, and in this economic climate we have to keep up with our receivables. We have noticed that you have made no payments for over 90 days, and so I must ask you, with regret, to make your future purchases on a cash basis until the account is cleared.

Please call or stop by the office if there is anything we can do to help resolve the situation. Meanwhile, I hope that things will turn around soon so we can all get back to normal.

Cordially,

Ed Marley

Ed Marley
Credit Manager

EBM/tgf

Sales Letter

"Junk mail" may be one of the nuisances of modern life, but it is also a powerful selling tool, with a quoted success rate of up to 5 percent.

With a sales letter, it's important to capture the reader's attention immediately (many direct mail letters have dollar bills printed on the envelope)!

Attention-Grabbing Openings

- Banner headline   MILLION DOLLAR PROMOTION

- Startling statistic   90% of our customers are millionaires

- Searching question   Have you ever dreamed of being a millionaire?

- Celebrity quote   "This product made me $1 million"
  —Donald Trump

- Human story   Joe Blow of Townsville wins $1 million!

Basic Structure

Strong Intro

Paragraph 1

Introduces the product

Paragraph 2

Enumerates benefits to buyer (*Remember*: features describe, benefits sell)

Paragraph 3

Presents call to action

The Magic Brush

55 Bristle Top   Strokes, TN 37920   (423) 555-9798

May 6, 2007

Robin Wright
Homedecor Ltd.
7374 Blue Lake Road
Wanabash, KS 67936

Dear Robin Wright:

TAKE THE "PAIN" OUT OF PAINTING!

As an interior design professional, you know the importance of quality tools for a quality finish. Now a brush is available that will take the "pain" out of painting forever more: *The Magic Brush.*

The Magic Brush is a revolutionary concept, using Compositron™ technology, Plastistrate™ paint, and the Graviflow™ system. Gone are days of drips and runs. You simply:

- Attach the Graviflow tank.
- Let the Plastistrate flow through the valve.
- Apply through the Compositron bristles for a clean and even finish!

Don't waste another minute with conventional paintbrushes. Simply dial 1-800-BRISTLE for your free trial or return the enclosed coupon. Act now and you can get *The Magic Brush* for only $99.99 while stock lasts. But hurry! They're disappearing—just like magic!

Sincerely,

Mark Potter

Mark Potter
Director of Sales and Marketing

Customer Appreciation

Customer appreciation letters are basically after-sales letters and come in two varieties:

- "Thanks for becoming a customer . . . "

  This letter is designed to counteract buyer's remorse (those second thoughts people sometimes have after making a purchase). The writer is saying:

  You did the right thing.

  You made the right choice.

  We are a sophisticated operation.

  We have a commitment to our customers.

  This letter is evidence of our after-sales service.

- "Thanks for remaining a customer . . . "

  This letter is designed to build brand loyalty—the tendency to stick with one name in products or services. Here the writer is saying:

  We go back a long way.

  You did make the right choice.

  We are a sophisticated operation.

  We have a commitment to our customers.

  See how we never forget you.

Both letters may also carry an "upsell" message: "Try another of our products!"

Basic Structure

Paragraph 1

Expresses congratulations or thanks

Paragraph 2

Draws attention to doing a great job

Paragraph 3

Promises to do as much as possible to serve the customer and upsells, if appropriate

Bull and Baer Inc., Stockbrokers

999 Wall Street, New York, New York 10083 (212) 555-2091

June 7, 2008

Mrs. Iris Stern
5035 Central Park South
New York, NY 10064

Dear Mrs. Stern:

On behalf of Bull and Baer Inc., I would like to thank you for your business over the past five years. Our association has been a successful one, and we look forward to the pleasure of your company for many years to come.

As one of the oldest money managers on Wall Street, our philosophy is "secure performance." Without exposing our clients to undue risk, we have managed to beat the market in seventy-nine of the last hundred years! You can be sure that your money will continue to grow safely with Bull and Baer Inc.

To enable you to monitor your assets from the comfort of your living room, Bull and Baer Inc. now offers "Market Online" to selected clients. For further information about this innovative service, please call me at 555-2091. In the meantime, I look forward to serving you in every way I can.

Yours very truly,

Bob Resch

Bob Resch
Investment Counselor

Invitation

There are three essential elements in a letter of invitation:

- Extension of invitation
- Notification of the event
- Notification of where/when

Basic Structure

Paragraph 1

Extends invitation

Paragraph 2

Identifies event/occasion

Paragraph 3

Specifies where/when event will take place

Key Phrases

In the case of a function, it is usual to start with:

"You are cordially invited . . . "

A more formal approach might be:

" . . . requests the pleasure of your company . . . "

Note

Another possibility is the guest speaker scenario, illustrated in the example that follows, where the actual invitation comes after the explanation.

Pilgrim College

1620 Mayflower Way, Stockade, New Hampshire 03450 (603) 555-0075

July 8, 2009

Dr. Ruth Vince
National Space Laboratory
2001 Harvard Yard
Boston, MA 02027

Dear Dr. Vince:

I have been following your *Science News* articles on extraterrestrial life with great interest. The possibility of life on Mars has always captivated the human imagination, and your research findings have suddenly brought it within the grasp of possibility.

Our science department at Pilgrim College offers a cosmology program that is very popular and well-supported. We currently have more than one hundred cosmology majors, and some of our alumni have gone on to work with NASA and other leading agencies.

On behalf of the college, I would be very grateful if you could take time out from your busy schedule to come and talk to us about your work. The date and time would be at your convenience between October 1 and December 10. All expenses and your honorarium would be met out of departmental funds.

I look forward to hearing from you.

Sincerely yours,

Egbert Varm

Egbert Varm
Dean of the Faculty of Science

Acknowledgment

The acknowledgment serves two main purposes:

- Providing an answer when the addressee is not available to answer

- Playing for time—if there is some doubt about whether to accept, if it's necessary to research the invitation further, or if someone needs to finalize the details of a tight schedule

Basic Structure

Paragraph 1

Expresses thanks for kind/gracious invitation

Paragraph 2

Provides explanation for delay

National Space Laboratory

2001 Harvard Yard, Boston, MA 02027 (617) 555-2010

July 12, 2009

Professor Egbert Varm
Dean of the Faculty of Science
Pilgrim College
1620 Mayflower Way
Stockade, NH 03450

Dear Professor Varm:

Thank you for your kind invitation to Dr. Ruth Vince to address the members of your institution on the subject of extraterrestrial life.

Dr. Vince is currently in Tokyo attending the International Cosmology Conference, from which she is expected to return on July 23. Please be assured that she will give your letter her prompt attention as soon as she is back at her desk.

Cordially yours,

David Trump

David Trump
Personal Assistant to Dr. Ruth Vince

Acceptance

The letter of acceptance serves two purposes:

1. Saying yes

2. Confirming arrangements

In the case of the sample letter, the arrangements have been left up to the invitee, so she will use the opportunity to pick her time.

Basic Structure

Paragraph 1

Expresses thanks for invitation, accepts, and confirms details

Paragraph 2

Notes any other information-relevant enclosures, preparatory work, and so on

Paragraph 3

Restates appreciation and mentions looking forward to occasion

National Space Laboratory

2001 Harvard Yard, Boston, MA 02027   (617) 555-2010

July 28, 2009

Professor Egbert Varm
Dean of the Faculty of Science
Pilgrim College
1620 Mayflower Way
Stockade, NH 03450

Dear Professor Varm:

Thank you for your kind invitation to address the Pilgrim College Faculty of Science. It will be my pleasure, and I would like to suggest Friday, October 25, at 10 a.m. Please let me know if that date presents a problem.

Recent developments in the field of cosmology have indeed been exciting, and I enclose my latest article on the Mars research. I also include the NSL honorarium schedule.

I appreciate your interest and I look forward to meeting with you, your faculty, and your students.

Sincerely,

Ruth Vince

Ruth Vince

RSV/dmt
Enclosures (2)

Invitation Refusal

Like all "bad news" letters, a refusal calls for tact and diplomacy. Not living up to the expectations of your fans is bad PR; therefore, the damage must be limited as much as possible, and you should find room for a few kind words.

Basic Structure

Paragraph 1

Expresses thanks for request and notes feeling honored by invitation

Paragraph 2

Provides reason for having to decline

Paragraph 3

Expresses encouragement/best wishes

Hints

1. Have a good excuse.

2. Make it somebody else's decision!

National Space Laboratory

2001 Harvard Yard, Boston, MA 02027 (617) 555-2010

July 28, 2009

Professor Egbert Varm
Dean of the Faculty of Science
Pilgrim College
1620 Mayflower Way
Stockade, NH 03450

Dear Professor Varm:

Thank you for your kind invitation to address the Pilgrim College Faculty of Science. I greatly appreciate your interest in my work, and I am flattered by your request.

Unfortunately, it is not the policy of the National Space Laboratory to accept speaking invitations from individual institutions. As you are aware, there are numerous schools around the country but only a small group of us working at the NSL. Our policy is to give priority to research, with as few interruptions as possible.

However, I am familiar with Pilgrim College and have been particularly impressed with your cosmology program. Please accept the enclosed copy of my latest article, *Solving the Martian Conundrum,* with my very best wishes.

Sincerely yours,

Ruth Vince

Ruth Vince

RSV/dmt

Enclosure

Job Application

The job application or résumé cover letter represents another kind of sales letter—this time selling yourself!

As in all sales letters, the assignment is the following:

- Get the reader's attention.
- Spell out the features and benefits.
- Make the call to action.

However, there are some differences:

- **Tone**

    The application calls for a certain blend of formality, politeness, and humility.

- **Organization**

    The first and last paragraphs are standard.

- **Presentation**

    Don't be afraid to use bullet points to highlight your features and benefits.

Basic Structure

Paragraph 1

States application for the post of (JOB) advertised on (DATE) in (PAPER)

Paragraph 2 (features and benefits)

Restates what employer needs (per ad) and describes how personal skills/experience would fit needs

Paragraph 3

Asserts good fit for position, mentions willingness to discuss application further/in person, expresses availability for interview, describes how to contact

1984 Plane Street
Hometon, OK 73856

August 9, 2010

Ms. Delores Panagopoulos
Human Resources Director
Baldwin Textiles, Inc.
9061 Ventura Highway
Pecan, CA 90610

Dear Ms. Panagopoulos:

I respectfully submit the enclosed résumé in application for the position of Office Manager as advertised today in *USA News*.

According to the specifications in the advertisement, you need an experienced, computer-literate administrator with bookkeeping and people skills. In the last five years, as Office Manager with Hometon Spinning Corp., my responsibilities have been:

- Coordinating the installation of a local area network.

- Introducing the "Office-Smart" bookkeeping system.

- Supervising all reception and secretarial functions.

- Directly managing twelve employees.

As my résumé indicates, I am a high school graduate with substantial experience. I believe I possess the necessary skills for an all-round administrator in a growing industry. I am also fully mobile and willing to relocate. I would be happy to discuss this application in person and can be contacted at (405) 555-0248.

Very truly yours,

Cybill Thornbush

Cybill Thornbush

Résumé

Although a résumé is not a letter, it very frequently accompanies a letter of application, so it is included here.

There are at least two schools of thought on résumés:

- **More is better.**

    Include every possible detail from "My objective is to find myself spiritually" to "My hobbies include butterfly collecting and macramé."

- **Exercise the "One Page Rule."**

Take your choice!

Essential

- **Heading**

    Name, address, phone, fax, e-mail

    All the information a potential employer needs to reach you

- **Experience**

    Work history in reverse chronological order

    Date - job title - employer

    Brief description of responsibilities (bullet for economy)

- **Qualifications** (can be listed before experience if appropriate)

    Education

    Training

Optional

- **Objective** (career goal)

  Focus goals on job you're applying for

  Use opportunity to list your strengths

- **Special Skills**

  Languages, computer skills, typing, etc.

- **Hobbies and Interests**

  Outside-of-work activities that strengthen your application

- **References**

  Perhaps hold these in reserve for when the employer asks for them

CYBILL THORNBUSH
1984 Plane Street
Hometon, OK 73856
Tel: (405) 555-0248
Fax: (405) 555-0249
E-mail: Cybill@oknet.com

OBJECTIVE:

To find a challenging administrative position that makes use of my technical and interpersonal skills

EXPERIENCE:

2005 - Present   Office Manager, Hometon Spinning Corp., Hometon, Oklahoma
- Managed administration department with 12 direct reports
- Supervised reception and secretarial functions
- Introduced Office-Smart bookkeeping system
- Coordinated local area network (LAN) installation

2003 - 2005   Accounts Supervisor, Office Warehouse, Bronco, Oklahoma
- Supervised five direct reports
- Responsible for accounts payable and accounts receivable
- Introduced Auto-Account tracking system

2001 - 2003   Accounts Clerk, Jack Harvester, Hometon, Oklahoma

1999 - 2001   Trainee Accounts Clerk, Jack Harvester, Hometon, Oklahoma

EDUCATION & TRAINING:

2002   Office Automation Course, Bronco Business College

1998 -1999   Secretarial Certificate, Bronco Business College
- Typing 80 w.p.m.
- Shorthand 120 w.p.m.

June 1998   Graduated Hometon High School, Hometon, Oklahoma

REFERENCES   Available on request

Reference

A letter of reference can be one of three things:

- A letter of recommendation
- A letter of reference
- A letter of condemnation (!!)

For example, a reference has been requested for Cybill Thornbush. Compare the following replies:

- Cybill Thornbush has been a key team member for five years, during which time she has made a great contribution, introducing new ideas, contributing beyond the call of duty . . .

- Cybill Thornbush has been an employee for five years, during which she performed her duties satisfactorily . . .

- Cybill Thornbush was employed here. Her attendance and punctuality were average.

As you can see, the message goes beyond the words themselves! Circumstances will dictate which of the three versions you write.

Basic Structure

Paragraph 1

Confirms period of employment and position held

Paragraph 2

Offers evaluation of performance

Paragraph 3

Offers additional information or telephone reference if required

Hometon Spinning Corp.

4040 Surrey Drive, Hometon, OK 73877 (405)555-5757

September 1, 2010

Delores Panagopoulos
Human Resources Director
Baldwin Textiles, Inc.
9061 Ventura Highway
Pecan, California 90610

Dear Ms. Panagopoulos:

It is my pleasure to confirm that Mrs. Cybill Thornbush has been employed by Hometon Spinning Corp. since 2005 in the position of Office Manager.

During that time she has made a valuable contribution to our Administration Division, with particular responsibility for the introduction of new office systems. She is a reliable and efficient manager, well-respected by her co-workers, and I recommend her highly.

Should you require further information, please feel free to contact me directly at (405) 555-5757.

Sincerely yours,

Edith Wharton

Edith Wharton
Personnel Director

Job Refusal

This is yet another of those "bad news" situations when you must choose your words very carefully (see the section on "Sincerity" in Part One).

Knowing that someone's pride is going to get hurt, you want to try to "be nice." Unfortunately, it is all too easy to sound phony.

On the other hand, you might be tempted to say the minimum to get it over with as quickly as possible. That is not advisable either—you could sound uncaring!

As with most things, moderation is the answer: not too short and not too sweet, just fair and honest.

Basic Structure

Paragraph 1

Expresses a thanks for application

Paragraph 2

Notes difficulty of decision as well as careful consideration resulting in job going to someone else

Paragraph 3

Expresses appreciation for submission and good luck for the future

Baldwin Textiles, Inc.

9061 Ventura Highway, Pecan, California 90610 (818) 555-1609

August 20, 2010

Ms. Cybill Thornbush
1984 Plane Street
Hometon, OK 73856

Dear Ms. Thornbush:

Thank you for your application for the position of Office Manager with
Baldwin Textiles, Inc.

Although we found your résumé impressive, we regret to inform you that the
position has been offered to a candidate whose background matched our
requirements more closely.

Baldwin Textiles appreciates your interest in applying, and we wish you every
success in your future endeavors.

Sincerely,

Delores Panagopoulos

Delores Panagopoulos
Human Resources Director

DPP/nyl

Congratulations

The letter of congratulation falls into the "social-business" category. It can be typed or handwritten.

Note also the comma after the salutation.

Two paragraphs are usually enough to say "well done."

Basic Structure

Paragraph 1

Expresses congratulations on [reason]

Mentions being thrilled/delighted

Paragraph 2

Extends wishes to whomever is celebrating with recipient and expresses willingness/extend offer to help in the future

Hometon Spinning Corp.

4040 Surrey Drive, Hometon, OK 73877 (405)555-5757

August 30, 2010

Dear Cybill,

Congratulations on your new position with Baldwin Textiles, Inc. of Pecan, California. You have done a great job here at Hometon Spinning and we are all going to miss you very much.

Please pass on our good wishes to Stanley. You have a great adventure ahead of you both in California. We'll be thinking of you!

Sincerely,

Bill

Condolences

Out of the blue, tragedy may strike a business associate or an employee. At such times, even though it may be hard to put pen to paper, the right thing to do is to send a letter of sympathy (condolence).

You can go to a store and buy a card that bears the message, but a personal note shows that extra bit of care and commitment.

The letter of condolence will normally come from the top, so it will often be printed on executive letterhead.

As with all "bad news" letters, the keynotes here are threefold:

- Simplicity
- Directness
- Sincerity

Basic Structure

Paragraph 1

Expresses (deep) sympathy at time of loss

Paragraph 2

Offers kind words about deceased

Paragraph 3

Extends offer of help/support

Hometon Spinning Corp.

4040 Surrey Drive, Hometon, OK 73877 (405)555-5757

OFFICE OF THE PRESIDENT

August 31, 2010

Dear Cybill:

On behalf of all your friends and co-workers at Hometon Spinning Corp., I would like to extend to you our deepest sympathies at this time of bereavement.

Many of us knew Stanley personally, and his presence will be missed by the entire community.

I want you to know that you have the support of us all, and if there is anything we can do, you know where to find us.

Sincerely,

Bill Barlow

Transmittal

A letter of transmittal is a covering letter with two main purposes:

- To serve as a notice for material sent under separate cover
- To accompany a report or other document

The transmittal letter adds a personal note to the formal structure of the document it accompanies.

Basic Structure

Paragraph 1

Identifies report, etc., enclosed or acknowledges request (for item sent under separate cover)

Paragraph 2

Describes method, scope, acknowledgments, etc., or materials sent under separate cover

Paragraph 3

Expresses thanks for opportunity and invites contact if questions arise

Note

The complimentary close reads *Respectfully submitted.*

THE APPLIED SCIENCE INSTITUTE

500 Nutrino Boulevard, Zircon Valley, OR 97301   (503) 555-2819

October 11, 2012

Ms. Sarah Fleming
Research Director
Peach Computers Limited
3000 Integral Way
Pinewood, OR 97430

Dear Ms. Fleming:

It gives me great pleasure to enclose our report Conductance, Conduction, and Conductivity.

As you requested, we have restricted the scope of the report to the areas you specified, incorporating the data from your earlier studies. Our research was based on extensive laboratory testing, and we would like to acknowledge the contributions of Professor Egbert Varm of Pilgrim College and Dr. Ruth Vince of the National Space Laboratory.

On behalf of The Applied Science Institute, I would like to thank you for the opportunity to work on this project. We are always happy when our scientific research can be put to use by local industry. If you have any questions regarding the report, please call me.

Respectfully submitted,

William Branson

William Branson, Ph.D.
Chief Scientific Officer

Part Four

Formatting Your Memos

Memos Versus Letters

What are the differences between memos and letters?

Here's a comparative list:

LETTER	MEMO
Outside the company	Inside the company
Different formats	One standard format
Polite and formal	Brief and to the point
No jargon allowed	Jargon allowed
Written on letterhead	Written on blank sheet or memo form
Inside address	No inside address
Salutation	No salutation
Complimentary close	No complimentary close

Exercise

Look at the two layouts that follow. Which is the letter and which is the memo?

XXXXXXXXX

XXXXXXXXX
XXXXXXXXX
XXXXXXXXX
XXXXXXXXX

XXXXXXXXX

XXXXXXXXXXXXXXXXXX

XXXXXXXXXXXXXXXXXXXXXXXXXXXXXXXXXXXXXXXXXXXXXXXXXXXXXXXXXXXX
XXXXXXXXXXXXXXXXXXXXXXXXXXXXXXXXXXXXXXXXXXXXXXXXXXXXXXXXXXXX
XXXXXXXXXXXXXXXXXXXXXXXXXXXXXXXXXXXXXXXXXXXXXXXXXXXXXXXXXXXX
XXXXXXXXXXXXXXXXXXXXXXXXXXXXXXXXXXXXXXXXX

XXXXXXXXXXXXXXXX

jegkuoekuhr

XXXXXXXXXX

xxxxxxxx xxxxxxxxxxxx
xxxxxxxx xxxxxxxxxxxx
xxxxxxx xxxxxxxxxxxx
xxxxxxx xxxxxxxxxxxxxxxxxxxxxx

xxxxxxxxxxxxxxxxxxxxxxxxxxxxxxxxxxxxxxxxxxxxxxxxxxxxxxxxx
xxxxxxxxxxxxxxxxxxxxxxxxxxxxxxxxxxxxxxxxxxxxxxxxxxxxxxxxx
xxxxxxxxxxxxxxxxxxxxxxxxxxxxxxxxxxxxxxxxxxxxxxxxxxxxxxxxx
xxxxxxxxxxxxxxxxxxxxxxxxxxxxxxxxxxxx

jegkuoekuhr

xxxxxxxxxxx

Parts of a Memo

Memos present a consistent format, containing the following parts (keyed numerically in the example on p. 133):

1. Head

Many companies and government organizations have printed forms for memos. Others either:

- Write "Memorandum" at the top, or

- Use a blank page and let the layout speak for itself.

2. "To"

This line, giving the name(s) of the addressee(s), serves both as inside address and as salutation.

3. "From"

This line replaces the return address on the letterhead, and in some cases also the signature block.

4. "Date"

In a memo, the date may be written in full or abbreviated (e.g., 1/1/11).

5. Subject Line

The subject line of a memo is very important:

- It should be concise yet explain the subject in full.

- It can act as the "beginning," reducing the body of the memo to two paragraphs—"middle" and "end."

6. Body

Two paragraphs should suffice:

- One giving the situation
- The second outlining the next step

7. Signature

Initials are OK in a memo.

8. Optional Parts

a. Initials of typist, or writer and typist

b. Enclosure notation

c. Copy notation

d. Security classification

e. File numbers

① INTEROFFICE MEMORANDUM

② **TO**	Judy White	⑧d **CLASSIFICATION**	Amber
③ **FROM**	Robert Brown	⑧e **OUR FILE**	R49A
④ **DATE**	1/1/11	⑧e **YOUR FILE**	R49B

⑤ **SUBJECT**	Departmental relocation

⑥

We are now ready to proceed with the relocation of Sections 1-4 to Hut 29, starting Monday. We hope to complete the exercise by the end of the week.

Please advise the Real Estate Dept. that all workers and equipment must be clear of the area by Saturday at the latest. Corporate Security will begin patrols at 12:01 Sunday. I enclose the necessary authorization codes.

⑦ *RB*

⑧a RB/gsd

⑧b Enc. (2)

⑧c cc: Jane Rae

Memo Language

Sometimes the language used in memos is different from the language used in letters. That is, what sounds "businesslike" in a memo might sound highhanded in a letter.

Tone

Letters

- Letters are addressed to people outside your organization.

- A letter is PR for your organization.

- The polite tone of your letters is a very important part of the message.

Memos

- Memos are addressed to people inside your organization.

- You are all working together for the good of the organization.

- Getting the message across quickly and clearly is the most important thing.

Clichés

Letters

Clichés are never a good idea in letters.

Memos

Clichés are not advisable in memos either, but certain stock phrases save time (a plus in the workplace) and point the reader in the right direction.

Jargon

Letters

Never put jargon in letters unless you're absolutely sure you are writing to someone who will understand and appreciate it.

Memos

Jargon is normal in memos; reader and writer work together, so obviously they will use their professional shorthand.

MEMORANDUM

FROM: Head Office

TO: All writers

DATE: 1/1/11

SUBJECT: Memo Language

With regard to memo language, you may be aware that certain stock phrases have come to our attention. Please note the following:

FOLLOWING UP
In connection with
Further to
With regard to
In response to
Concerning

POINTING TO EXISTING INFORMATION
As you are aware
As you may be aware
As you are no doubt aware
As you know
As you may already know
You may recall

INTRODUCING NEW INFORMATION
It has been brought to my attention
It has come to my attention

POINTING OUT
Your attention is directed to
I would like to direct your attention to
I would like to point out
Please note
It should be noted that

EXPRESSING UNDERSTANDING
It is my understanding
I understand
It is understood
We recognize
It is recognized
We appreciate
It is appreciated

Part Five

Sample Memos

Action

The action memo can be:

- An instruction.
- The green light to a prearranged plan.
- An attempt to speed things up.

Basic Structure

Subject

States the matter at hand

Paragraph 1

Announces decision to act, with background included as necessary/appropriate

Paragraph 2

Advises recipient(s) to take the next step and/or to expedite as soon as possible

Note

Use capital letters for organizational terms (Department, Section) and bullets to list items clearly and economically.

MEMORANDUM

TO: Danielle Gould
FROM: Jeremy Dean
DATE : 1/2/03

SUBJECT: Departmental cost-cutting initiative

Spending exceeded budgetary projections by a large margin in the last fiscal year. It has therefore been decided that a general cost-cutting initiative must be implemented immediately by all Departments.

I am asking all Section Heads to submit a list of cost-cutting suggestions in support of this initiative. The areas that should be examined are:

- Manpower.
- Materials.
- Equipment.
- Energy.

The list should be submitted to me by 9:00 a.m. Friday for review at the Department meeting Monday morning.

Announcement

The announcement memo resembles a news flash. It usually appears when there has been a major change, such as the following:

- New hire
- New product
- Reorganization

Basic Structure

Subject

Announces the matter at hand

Paragraph 1

States what the boss/company/department is pleased/proud to announce, identifies when this news becomes effective, and supplies any other important details

Paragraph 2

Rallies recipients to join in welcoming/supporting, and so on

MEMORANDUM

TO: All Staff
FROM: Vice President
DATE: 2/2/02

SUBJECT: <u>Appointment of Service Manager</u>

We are pleased to announce the appointment of Dick Ward as our new Service Manager, effective immediately. Dick comes to us from Island Autos, where he headed the service division for three years. He and his family are relocating to the area, and I know they will be an asset to the community.

Please join us in extending a warm welcome to Dick and his family, and in offering him full cooperation and support in his new position.

Appreciation

Appreciation memos present a pat on the back to people who have pulled off a major piece of business or gone that extra mile for the organization. These communications build morale, show that management cares about employees' efforts, and prompt even greater efforts in the future.

Basic Structure

Subject

Announces achievement, reason for congratulations, and so on

Paragraph 1

Identifies on behalf of and to who thanks or congratulations are expressed and for what action/achievement

Paragraph 2

Offers praise, notes example set, repeats thanks/congratulations

Note

Don't use the same words for "congratulations," "thanks," and so forth in both paragraphs. For example, write "congratulations" in paragraph 1 and "thanks" in paragraph 2.

MEMORANDUM

TO: All staff
FROM: President
DATE: 3/3/03

SUBJECT: Employee of the Year

On behalf of Union Cookies Inc., I would like to take this opportunity to congratulate Bobbie Hernandez, who has been named Employee of the Year. She has consistently set an example of hard work, dedication to the company, a positive attitude, and quality customer service.

Because of people like you, Bobbie, Union Cookies is number one in the industry. Where would we be without you? Thank you for all your efforts, and keep up the good work!

Approval

Memos provide the perfect vehicle for the traffic of ideas and instructions within an organization. Among other advantages, they provide a permanent record of communications, which helps avoid misunderstandings such as "Nobody told us."

The approval memo somewhat resembles the action memo. Specifically, it gives the go-ahead to a suggestion or request and thus becomes a valuable record. If anything goes wrong, the authority for the action is there in black and white.

Basic Structure

Subject

Names proposal, suggestion, request, and so forth

Paragraph 1

Confirms review of proposal/suggestion/request and decision to approve

Paragraph 2

Gives OK to proceed to next step

MEMORANDUM

TO: Sharon Crowe
FROM: Personnel Dept.
DATE: 4/4/04

SUBJECT: Application for study leave

This is to advise you that your study leave application has been reviewed, and approval is granted.

Under company policy, you are required to submit the following documents:

- College prospectus
- Syllabus specification
- Schedule of tuition fees
- Academic calendar

As soon as these have been received, the necessary authorizations will be issued.

RW

Evaluation

The evaluation memo offers an opinion on some new initiative, product, and so forth. It is part of the process of turning ideas into action.

The most important aspect of the evaluation memo is the reasoning behind it.

Basic Structure

Subject

Identifies concept under consideration

Paragraph 1

Announces completion of examination/study/review

Paragraph 2

Offers comments and conclusion

MEMORANDUM

TO: Operations Dept.
FROM: Workshop Safety Review Committee
DATE: 5/5/05

SUBJECT: Workshop safety posters

This is to advise you that the Committee has now completed its review of the proposed safety posters submitted by the Worksafe Agency.

The findings of the Committee were as follows:

- The proposed size is too small to give the necessary prominence.

- The colors do not show up well under workshop lighting.

- The slogans may not be understood by some of the employees.

The Committee therefore concluded that the Worksafe Agency posters are incompatible with the specified safety requirements and an alternative proposal should be sought as soon as possible.

RAF
PIA
RB

Information

Like the announcement, the information memo is a kind of news bulletin.

Its main functions are to:

- Get the word out.

- Get the word out as quickly as possible.

- Get the word out to everyone.

- Get the word on paper so that no one can say he or she didn't know.

In structure, the announcement resembles the action memo.

Basic Structure

Subject

Identifies news item

Paragraph 1

Articulates announcement

Paragraph 2 (if needed)

Explains next step or necessary action

MEMORANDUM

TO: All employees
FROM: Head Office
DATE: 6/6/06

SUBJECT: Production Line Shutdown

Please note that the production line will be shut down for twenty-four hours on July 1 to allow maintenance work on the main generator set.

All production line workers should report for duty as normal, as a major cleanup of the assembly area and related facilities has been scheduled for that day. A wiener roast will be provided at lunch time, courtesy of management.

HO

Refusal

A refusal is the reverse of an approval memo. Where the approval lists the next steps, the refusal gives reasons.

Paragraph 1 resembles the approval memo; paragraph 2 resembles the evaluation memo.

Basic Structure

Paragraph 1

Advises that request/application has been reviewed

Paragraph 2

States inability to approve and provides reasons why

MEMORANDUM

TO;   Kim John
FROM: Murray McDonald
DATE: 7/7/07

SUBJECT: <u>Reduction in Branch Opening Hours</u>

Your request for a reduction in Branch opening hours has been given careful consideration by Retail Division.

We acknowledge that you made a strong case, but unfortunately we are not in a position to approve operational changes for the moment. Our market research surveys indicate that the convenience factor is good for customer loyalty. We are not convinced the manpower cost savings outweigh the public relations benefits at this time. However, we do thank you for your suggestion and assure you we will be keeping a close eye on the situation.

MGM

Reprimand

A written reprimand is a built-in feature, usually the first or second step, in a modern human resources disciplinary structure. There may be specialized formats for an official reprimand, but remember: if it's on paper, it's on file!

Basic Structure

Subject

Identifies outcome or event triggering the reprimand

Paragraph 1

Sets scene, detailing events leading up to the problem and how it came to light

Paragraph 2

Expresses disapproval, possibly followed by a warning or threat

Note

Special care is needed to ensure the reprimand does not go beyond the guidelines of human resources procedure.

MEMORANDUM

TO: Isaac Oldham

FROM: Human Resources

DATE: 8/8/08

SUBJECT: <u>Damage to Conveyor Belt B</u>

On August 6, a plastic sandwich box was conveyed into the primary gear cluster of Conveyor Belt B, causing a substantial amount of damage and closing down the production line for more than three hours. The initials on the sandwich box, "I.O.," identify it as your property, and video footage from our internal security cameras show you in the act of falling asleep, allowing the box to fall onto the belt.

Company regulation 39f states: "No employee shall eat or be in possession of food in any operational area." Company regulation 102a states: "No employee shall be asleep while in control of operational equipment." You were in violation of both regulations, and this memorandum is to advise you that any future breach of company regulations will result in immediate termination of your employment.

HR

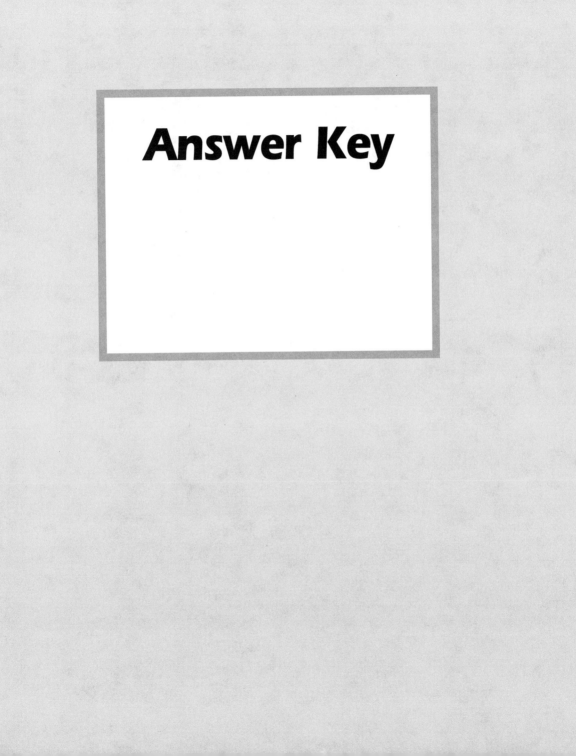

Answer Key

Clichés (p. 6)

1. We are in receipt of
2. Pleased be advised
3. in regard to the above mentioned
4. pursuant to
5. please find enclosed
6. your further advices
7. please do not hesitate to

Redundancy (p. 9)

1. completely fill
2. this moment in time
3. reason is because
4. advance planning
5. surplus left over
6. gathered together
7. basic essentials
8. consensus of opinion
9. vast majority
10. therein . . . within
11. past experience
12. brief in duration
13. a period of . . . two weeks
14. about approximately

15. return back

16. truly sincerely

Viewpoint (p. 21)

First-person references: Letter A-9, Letter B-0

Second-person references: Letter A-0, Letter B-6

Sentences and Paragraphs (p. 30)

1. Sentence 1 has five clauses—three too many.

2. Paragraph 2 has the topic sentence last; it should be first.

3. Paragraph 3, sentence 1 has no verb.

4. Paragraph 3, sentence 2 has commas in the middle of clauses.

5. Paragraph 3, sentence 3 has no main verb—can what?

6. "Look forward" has no subject.

Accuracy (p. 33)

1. Typo: main Street

2. Spelling: recieved

3. Factual: June 31

4. Spelling: Unfortunatly

5. Spelling: buisness

6. Factual: New York . . . nation's capital

7. Punctuation: but, as soon as

8. Typo: he return

9. Spelling: Sincerly

10. Typo: Ann White

Parts of a Letter (p. 38)

A = 12

B = 6

C = 9

D = 10

E = 2

F = 4

G = 5

H = 1

I = 13

J = 3

K = 7

L = 11

M = 8

Inside Address (p. 51)

1. Edwin (Edward)

2. M.S.C. (M.Sc.)

3. Chairman (President)

4. Clinical Department (Clinical Division)

5. Pharmaceuticals (Pharmaceutical Products)

6. Ltd. (Limited)

7. Unit # 3 (Unit 3)

8. 73890 (98290)

Salutation (p. 57)

A. Dear Doctors:

B. Dear Marion Morrissey:

C. Dear Governors:

D. Dear Mrs. Brown:

E. Gentlemen:

Complimentary Close (p. 59)

A. 5

B. 3

C. 1

D. 2

E. 4

Signature Block (p. 61)

A. Judy Harrison

B. Personal Assistant to Dr. Winston Smith

C. WS/wmh

D. Enclosures (5)

E. Dr. William Jones

Bibliography
and
Suggested
Reading

Baugh, L. Sue, Maridell Fryar, and David A. Thomas. *How to Write First-Class Business Correspondence*. Lincolnwood, IL: NTC, 1995.

Blake, Gary. *Quick Tips for Better Business Writing*. New York: McGraw-Hill, 1995.

Davies, Dave. *Grammar? No Problem!* Mission, KS: SkillPath Publications, 1997.

Davies, David, and G. D. Pickett. *English for Commerce*. Englewood Cliffs, NJ: Prentice Hall, 1990.

Freeman, Lawrence H., and Terry R. Bacon. *Style Guide*. Bountiful, UT: Shipley Associates, 1994.

Geffner, Andrea B. *Business Letters the Easy Way*. Hauppage, NY: Barron's, 1991.

Kipfer, Barbara Ann. *21st Century Manual of Style*. New York: Laurel, 1993.

Kramer, Melinda G., Glenn Leggett, and C. David Mead. *Prentice Hall Handbook for Writers*. Englewood Cliffs, NJ: Prentice Hall, 1995.

Lindsell-Roberts, Sheryl. *Merriam-Webster's Secretarial Handbook*. Springfield, MA: Merriam-Webster, 1993.

Sabin, William A. *The Gregg Reference Manual*. Lake Forest, IL: Glencoe, 1992.

Trace, Jacqueline. *Style and Strategy of the Business Letter*. Englewood Cliffs, NJ: Prentice Hall, 1985.

Available From SkillPath Publications

Self-Study Sourcebooks

Climbing the Corporate Ladder: What You Need to Know and Do to Be a Promotable Person *by Barbara Pachter and Marjorie Brody*

Coping With Supervisory Nightmares: 12 Common Nightmares of Leadership and What You Can Do About Them *by Michael and Deborah Singer Dobson*

Defeating Procrastination: 52 Fail-Safe Tips for Keeping Time on Your Side *by Marlene Caroselli, Ed.D.*

Discovering Your Purpose *by Ivy Haley*

Going for the Gold: Winning the Gold Medal for Financial Independence *by Lesley D. Bissett, CFP*

Having Something to Say When You Have to Say Something: The Art of Organizing Your Presentation *by Randy Horn*

Info-Flood: How to Swim in a Sea of Information Without Going Under *by Marlene Caroselli, Ed.D.*

The Innovative Secretary *by Marlene Caroselli, Ed.D.*

Letters & Memos: Just Like That! *by Dave Davies*

Mastering the Art of Communication: Your Keys to Developing a More Effective Personal Style *by Michelle Fairfield Poley*

Obstacle Illusions: Coverting Crisis to Opportunity *by Marlene Caroselli, Ed.D.*

Organized for Success! 95 Tips for Taking Control of Your Time, Your Space, and Your Life *by Nanci McGraw*

A Passion to Lead! How to Develop Your Natural Leadership Ability *y Michael Plumstead*

P.E.R.S.U.A.D.E.: Communication Strategies That Move People to Action *by Marlene Caroselli, Ed.D.*

Productivity Power: 250 Great Ideas for Being More Productive *by Jim Temme*

Promoting Yourself: 50 Ways to Increase Your Prestige, Power, and Paycheck *by Marlene Caroselli, Ed.D.*

Proof Positive: How to Find Errors Before They Embarrass You *by Karen L. Anderson*

Risk-Taking: 50 Ways to Turn Risks Into Rewards *by Marlene Caroselli, Ed.D. and David Harris*

Stress Control: How You Can Find Relief From Life's Daily Stress *by Steve Bell*

The Technical Writer's Guide *by Robert McGraw*

Total Quality Customer Service: How to Make It Your Way of Life *by Jim Temme*

Write It Right! A Guide for Clear and Correct Writing *by Richard Andersen and Helene Hinis*

Your Total Communication Image *by Janet Signe Olson, Ph.D.*

Handbooks

The ABC's of Empowered Teams: Building Blocks for Success *by Mark Towers*

Assert Yourself! Developing Power-Packed Communication Skills to Make Your Points Clearly, Confidently, and Persuasively *by Lisa Contini*

Breaking the Ice: How to Improve Your On-the-Spot Communication Skills *by Deborah Shouse*

The Care and Keeping of Customers: A Treasury of Facts, Tips, and Proven Techniques for Keeping Your Customers Coming BACK! *by Roy Lantz*

Challenging Change: Five Steps for Dealing With Change *by Holly DeForest and Mary Steinberg*

Dynamic Delegation: A Manager's Guide for Active Empowerment *by Mark Towers*

Every Woman's Guide to Career Success *by Denise M. Dudley*

Exploring Personality Styles: A Guide for Better Understanding Yourself and Your Colleagues *by Michael Dobson*

Grammar? No Problem! *by Dave Davies*

Great Openings and Closings: 28 Ways to Launch and Land Your Presentations With Punch, Power, and Pizazz *by Mari Pat Varga*

Hiring and Firing: What Every Manager Needs to Know *by Marlene Caroselli, Ed.D. with Laura Wyeth, Ms.Ed.*

How to Be a More Effective Group Communicator: Finding Your Role and Boosting Your Confidence in Group Situations *by Deborah Shouse*

How to Deal With Difficult People *by Paul Friedman*

Learning to Laugh at Work: The Power of Humor in the Workplace *by Robert McGraw*

Making Your Mark: How to Develop a Personal Marketing Plan for Becoming More Visible and More Appreciated at Work *by Deborah Shouse*

Meetings That Work *by Marlene Caroselli, Ed.D.*

The Mentoring Advantage: How to Help Your Career Soar to New Heights *by Pam Grout*

Minding Your Business Manners: Etiquette Tips for Presenting Yourself Professionally in Every Business Situation *by Marjorie Brody and Barbara Pachter*

Misspeller's Guide *by Joel and Ruth Schroeder*

Motivation in the Workplace: How to Motivate Workers to Peak Performance and Productivity *by Barbara Fielder*

NameTags Plus: Games You Can Play When People Don't Know What to Say *by Deborah Shouse*

Networking: How to Creatively Tap Your People Resources *by Colleen Clarke*

New & Improved! 25 Ways to Be More Creative and More Effective *by Pam Grout*

Power Write! A Practical Guide to Words That Work *by Helene Hinis*

The Power of Positivity: Eighty ways to energize your life *by Joel and Ruth Schroeder*

Putting Anger to Work For You *by Ruth and Joel Schroeder*

Reinventing Your Self: 28 Strategies for Coping With Change *by Mark Towers*

Saying "No" to Negativity: How to Manage Negativity in Yourself, Your Boss, and Your Co-Workers *by Zoie Kaye*

The Supervisor's Guide: The Everyday Guide to Coordinating People and Tasks *by Jerry Brown and Denise Dudley, Ph.D.*

Taking Charge: A Personal Guide to Managing Projects and Priorities *by Michal E. Feder*

Treasure Hunt: 10 Stepping Stones to a New and More Confident You! *by Pam Grout*

A Winning Attitude: How to Develop Your Most Important Asset! *by Michelle Fairfield Poley*

For more information, call 1-800-873-7545.